PLEASE HELP US TO PROTEC

C000175953

A few words about walking and access on Bc the enactment of the CRoW Act. There are that are unfenced and known as common land may walk anywhere we wish. The "common" rights of certain farmers to graze their animals upon these areas – common grazing rights. Most, if not all, of Bodmin Moor is in private ownership, which obviously means that permission should be sought before walking across it. We must keep to recognised rights of way and remember that a permissive path is just that – a route for which permission has been given for you to walk on a temporary basis and which may be closed should circumstances change and the landowner wishes to do so.

Please adhere to the countryside code:

- Be safe – plan ahead and follow any signs
- Leave gates and property as you find them
- Protect plants and animals and take your litter home
- Keep dogs under close control
- Consider other people

A fully explained version of the newly revised countryside code can be found on **www.countrysideaccess.gov.uk**, email **openaccess@countryside.gov.uk** or telephone 0845 100 3298.

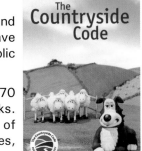

Busy traffic on small country roads can be unpleasant and dangerous to all – so slow down and, where possible, leave your vehicle at home, consider sharing lifts and using public transport or cycling.

For public transport information phone Traveline on 0870 608 2608 or visit the above website for useful links. Corlink is a bus service that operates on the west side of the moor – it operates like a taxi but charges bus fares, please ring 0845 850 5556 to use this excellent service.

For high quality, independently inspected accommodation on Bodmin Moor, please visit www.bobm.info.

Paul Glendell, © The Countryside Agency

The Best of Bodmin Moor

The Copper Trail

The idea of creating a circular walk around Bodmin Moor was something I had been mulling over for some time. Walkers come to Cornwall in their thousands every year to walk the South West Coast Path, but how many ever think about exploring the inland areas? Away from the gift shops and fast food outlets that often blight many of the seaside towns and villages there is another Cornwall waiting to be discovered. This other Cornwall remains hidden, even to many who live in the County.

Working with The Best of Bodmin Moor, I have been able to realise this ambition and create what I consider to be the best possible circular walk of the moor. It has not been without its difficulties and I hope you will understand when you have to take what looks like a pointless detour, that there is a reason for it. Avoiding busy roads....unwalkable or blocked paths....no legal access...only some of the problems that I have had to meander around.

The name 'The Copper Trail' comes about because of the great number of abandoned mines that are passed along the route. Not all are as visible as the ones encountered around Minions. In fact many have disappeared back into the ground from which they rose. Many of the paths on this trail originated as ways to get to and from work. They serve as a reminder of a time when the moor was alive with industry and activity.

The trail covers about 60 miles and I have split it into 6 sections that each should be possible to walk in a day. Although I have started at Minions you are free to start wherever you like. If you wish to do the whole trail you will need to consider suitable accommodation stops along the way. This may influence the length of each day's walk. You are advised to carry a copy of the OS map for Bodmin Moor (Explorer™ 109) which covers the area of the complete route.

Whichever way you do the trail, I hope you enjoy it as much as I have whilst creating it. Wonderful scenery and some great places to visit all provide interest along the route. I have tried to give details about various points of interest that you will come across, but realise that I have not covered everything. That would need a book three or four times the size of this one!

As always, enjoy your walking.

Mark Camp

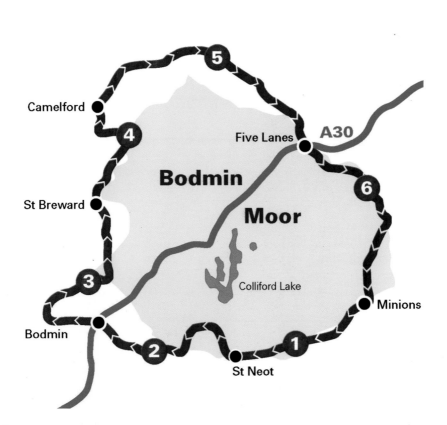

Day 1
Minions to St Neot
8½ miles

TO SIBLY BACK

TO SIBLY BACK

COMMON MOOR

TO DRAYNES

CAR PARK & W.C.

GOLITHA FALLS

RIVER FOWEY

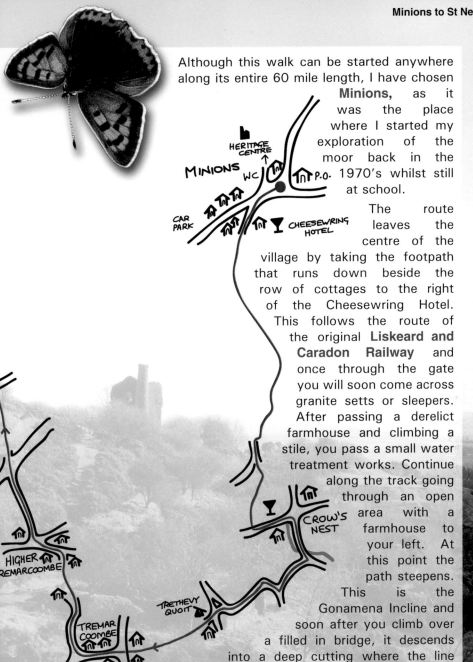

Although this walk can be started anywhere along its entire 60 mile length, I have chosen **Minions,** as it was the place where I started my exploration of the moor back in the 1970's whilst still at school.

The route leaves the centre of the village by taking the footpath that runs down beside the row of cottages to the right of the Cheesewring Hotel. This follows the route of the original **Liskeard and Caradon Railway** and once through the gate you will soon come across granite setts or sleepers. After passing a derelict farmhouse and climbing a stile, you pass a small water treatment works. Continue along the track going through an open area with a farmhouse to your left. At this point the path steepens. This is the Gonamena Incline and soon after you climb over a filled in bridge, it descends into a deep cutting where the line splits to allow wagons to pass.

When you leave the cutting you suddenly find yourself amongst the remains of one of

Minions:

If you look on the original OS maps of the early 1800s you will find no trace of Minions. It didn't exist. It was only with the discovery of copper on nearby Caradon Hill in the 1840s that people started to populate this high moorland area. Even then the name Minions didn't exist, the village being known as Cheesewring Village into the early 20th Century.

That's not to say people had not lived here before. All around the village are the remains of prehistoric life. The Hurlers stone circles lie just to the west, three circles dating back to the early Bronze Age. Nearby is the Rillaton Barrow, a burial site which when excavated in the mid 1800s was found to contain a gold cup; one of England's most treasured prehistoric finds. More barrows can be found on the summit of Caradon Hill overlooking the village, whilst further afield all sorts of evidence of man's early occupation of the moor is waiting to be discovered by those of a curious nature.

The village itself centres on the Cheesewring Hotel, Post Office/ General store and Hurlers Halt tea shop. All offer refreshments for the needy walker. At one time the railway ran straight through the centre of the village. Now you are more likely to see sheep or cattle strolling along the road, oblivious to modern traffic. It is a reminder, if needed, that you are on the moor proper here, with no enclosed fields, just open moorland stretching away...... waiting to be explored.

Liskeard and Caradon Railway:

This was built in the 1840s to serve the mines and granite quarries of the Minions area. Heavy wagons full of stone and ore

would use gravity to run down to Moorswater below Liskeard. There the cargo would be transferred onto barges before making its slow journey down the six mile long Liskeard and Looe Canal.

With mining production intensifying, the canal company took the decision to build a railway alongside the canal in the 1850s. Shortly after this an extension to the mineral line up onto the moors was diverted around Caradon Hill. This allowed steam trains to access the mines via an easier route and this steep stretch, known as the Gonamena Incline, was abandoned.

Following the closure of most of the mines in the area by the late 1800s the railway struggled on. Granite was still being quarried and sent out from the port at Looe, and the occasional Sunday school excursion brought children up onto the wild moors. But the

the richest mining areas of East Cornwall. On the other side of the valley lies **South Caradon Mine**, its ruined engine houses standing proud amongst the bracken and spoil tips. The footpath takes you up amongst the waste tips of West Caradon, a barren landscape where occasionally you may come across a piece of copper ore or a lump of fool's gold. The higher you climb, the more of South Caradon Mine can be seen, as well as views out over East Cornwall to the sea.

Eventually the path brings you up to Downhill Farm where it skirts the garden to join the track to the left of the cattle grid. From here proceed downhill for a while, passing over a silted up cattlegrid before soon turning left down a bridleway. As you descend you will twice cross the old railway lines that took the copper ore and granite down to Looe. A plan was put forward a few years ago to create a recreational trail along the old route, but this had to be cancelled because much of the land has now been "incorporated"

The Hurlers

Trethevy Quoit

outbreak of war in 1914 signalled the end of the line - much of it was taken up and sent out to the battlefields of France, leaving just the stone setts to mark its serpentine course.

South Caradon Mine:

It was here in 1836 that the boom in copper mining in the Minions area started. Standing on the western side of Caradon Hill are the remains of man's endeavours to persuade the land of Cornwall to give up its hidden riches. In the 50 years that the mine was worked, over 200,000 tons of ore was lifted out of this hillside. The buildings that housed the engines necessary for the job still stand proud amongst the gorse.

What is left to see is only a fraction of what there once was, and projects are in place to make sure that nothing else is lost from what was one of the most important industrial sites in Cornwall.

Trethevy Quoit:

Hidden behind hedges and houses, this spectacular edifice can be easily missed. It is possibly Cornwall's oldest man made structure with some experts dating its construction to 4,500 B.C. It is a tomb, but for whom we do not know. It may even have been for more than one person. When it was originally built, it would have been covered in earth, but this eroded away many years ago. As with so many of the ancient remains dotted around Cornwall, any evidence of its use had been removed long before archaeologists were "invented".

into local gardens. When you reach the road, turn left. After a short walk you will find the Crow's Nest Inn; time for some refreshments?

Leave the village by taking the lane on the right just past the Inn. This follows the Seaton River for a short while before bearing right just before Trenouth, a former mill. The lane climbs up past Trethevy Farm to **Trethevy Quoit** and the small community that has grown up around it. A bridleway leads down between the Quoit and the cottages. It is known locally as "Roman Lane"

St Cleer:

Just off the route lies the village of St Cleer with its church and Holy Well. It also has two pubs to refresh the tired walker and a post office and shop for supplies.

ıul Glendell, © *The Countryside Agency*

The church dates back to the 13th Century, although it is built on the remains of a Norman site (a blocked up door still remains). Its 15th Century tower can be seen from quite some distance, helped by the fact that it rises nearly 100ft above the village. Inside the church the most interesting features are the text boards dating back to 1662. There are 12 of these, the only examples in Cornwall and also a rarity in other parts of the country.

Before you reach the church you will pass the Holy well, enclosed in its own little courtyard. The waters are said to have the power or "Monks Walk" though no-one knows why. At the bottom of the lane you arrive in Tremar Coombe. Go straight across the road and head uphill. As you leave the houses, the village of **St Cleer** comes into view. To visit the village and its Holy Well, carry on when the road bends round to the left, otherwise turn right up the lane to Trecarne Farm.

Follow the lane around to the right in front of Old Trecarne Farmhouse and on to its end where the footpath carries on through Trecarne farmyard, passing between the barns on the right and the farmhouse on the left. You once again cross the old railway line before the path climbs up over rough pasture. Keeping to the right hand side hedge, you will eventually arrive at a rough track which leads to the road at Higher Tremarcoombe. Turn left at the road and walk up to the junction, cross here and carry straight on up the narrow lane. The next road you meet is the main Minions-Dobwalls road and care should be taken crossing it. Once over, go through the gate and follow the track. Just before Little Barton is reached, take

the path that goes off to the right. This brings you out onto the lane to Great Gimble, where you turn left.

Follow the lane as it crosses a cattle grid and descends to a gate beside a pond. Here the road divides. Take the left hand side path that goes through a gate, past the barn and then in front of Gimble Mill. From here continue down the valley following the waymarked path. After a couple of fields you will come to a stile and a footbridge. Go over these and pick your way through the gorse bushes to a large open space. Continue in the same direction and you will soon meet a path coming in from the right. A diversion can be taken here to visit **Siblyback Reservoir** where refreshments can be taken.

By following the raised track left you will come to a gate and once through it you find yourself on the edge of Common Moor village. After a few yards, and just before the cottage called Torview, take a little path on the right. A little gate marked No Cycling or Horse Riding opens to reveal a narrow path beside the stream. At times the stream is the path, so be prepared to get wet feet if you are not careful. An alternative route through the village does not take you too far out of the way. In summer this path is full of Himalayan balsam, a plant which the Victorians imported for their gardens, but which

Gimble Mill Pond

has now escaped and become naturalised alongside many streams in East Cornwall. The path leaves the stream by a large wall and runs alongside gardens to a road where you now turn right. You pass a row of cottages with hardly any windows in the back walls, before the lane comes to a sudden end. A stone footbridge leads to a gate and once again you are following the little stream as it twists and turns between the fields.

A road is met once again at South Trekeive, cross it and follow the footpath on the other side. This takes you over a couple of stiles and then follows the stream towards the water treatment works. Go through an old kissing gate to the right and rejoin the stream at the other end. Soon the path forks as you reach the woodland. Keep to the right where you will find stone steps taking you over a wall and into the scrubland. Gorse and small trees line the route as it twists and turns alongside the stream. After a while the valley opens out to your left and an area of marshy land appears. This area is great for bird watching but although a footpath is marked

to cure insanity although access to them is now prevented by a metal grill. The building around the well dates back to the 15th Century, but by the time the author Wilkie Collins visited the well in the mid 1800s it was in a sorry state. Only one arched wall stood in place, overgrown with ivy, and the local lads sat around on the fallen stones whistling where their ancestors had once knelt in prayer.

Siblyback Reservoir:

Created in 1969, an area of about 140 acres is covered by the reservoir, which is now managed by the South West Lakes Trust and used as a centre for waterborne activities. The whole reservoir can be walked around on a good path, and refreshments can be gained at the café which overlooks it.

Golitha Falls and the River Fowey:

The only time on this walk that we cross the River Fowey is at Draynes Bridge, after which it descends off the moor's edge at Golitha Falls. The name Golitha is thought to mean obstacle and a large boulder that once blocked a part of the river was blown up in the 19th Century to allow salmon upstream to spawn. Now a popular spot for walkers and strollers, the area is managed by English Nature, who try to keep a balance between a recreational site and an important wildlife area.

Hidden amongst the ferns and lichens that thrive in the moist conditions are the remains of a short lived mining operation, with two large wheel pits sitting on the side of the valley at the head of the falls. Another industrial remnant is the pipe that used to carry china clay slurry from Parson's Park above St Neot to the dries below Liskeard. It can be seen crossing the river only a short distance from the entrance to the woods.

The River Fowey rises high on the moor below Brown Willy, the highest hill. Medieval travellers knew the moor as Foweymoor, just as the rivers Dart and Exe give their names to their respective moors. It runs down through the Draynes valley to Golitha, a valley that was threatened with flooding when plans for a reservoir were put forward in the early 1970s. In the end another reservoir was built just to the west at Colliford and the valley was saved.

After Golitha the river increases in size as it runs down towards Lostwithiel, once an important port and capital of Cornwall. Nowadays boats can only reach the town on high tides and it is Fowey, the port that took the river's name, that is now known for its deep harbour and china clay docks.

Draynes Bridge

carry on down the lane the wooded valley of the Fowey can be glimpsed through gateways on the right. A tributary of it is crossed at the bottom of the hill at Trenant where the old **Methodist Chapel** has been converted into a private residence.

Go past the chapel and turn right through a gate into a field. Follow the hedge on your right to another gate into Periock Wood. The path now climbs up through mixed woodland with the stream falling down through a mini gorge on your right. This is part of the Two Valleys Walk, a circular walk from St Neot and is easily followed by signposts. After crossing a couple of fields the path once again enters woodland before climbing to the road at South Bowden. Turn right here along the road towards Northwood. At the top of the hill there is a wood on the right. Opposite is a gate leading onto open moorland, go through it. From up here there are good views to

as crossing it on the map, I would keep to the signed route.

When you reach a gate and the road, turn left and walk down the road to Draynes Bridge. Turn right over the bridge. **Golitha Falls** is a popular walking spot for locals and tourists alike, and well worth a detour if you have the time. There are also public toilets here.

The route from here takes you along a country lane for a mile or so. At first the road runs between Golitha Woods and the river, but soon it starts inevitably to climb. After passing the turnings to Great Draynes Farm and South Draynes it starts to level out and descends to the hamlet of Draynes itself. As you

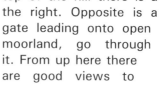

Potentilla erecta
TORMENTIL

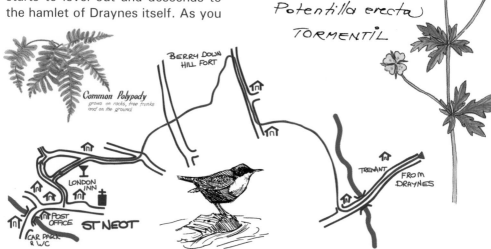

Common Polypody
grows on rocks, tree trunks and on the ground

BERRY DOWN HILL FORT

LONDON INN

POST OFFICE
ST NEOT

CAR PARK & WC

TRENANT
FROM DRAYNES

Trenant Memorial

Trenant Methodist Chapel:

Like many Methodist chapels in Cornwall this one has been converted into a private dwelling. It was built in 1826 and served the scattered community from St Neot to Golitha, many of them miners. By the 1960s the community had dwindled and the Methodists amongst them were few. The little chapel was closed and became a store for farm machinery.

Beside the chapel, and apparently private land, sits the graveyard. The large monument in the corner nearest the road belongs to Jim Eva, a local who was said to be in league with the devil. Because of this, when he died, the locals had this huge lump of stone placed on top of him...to keep him down!

Parson's Park China Clay Works:

China clay (kaolin) was first extracted from Bodmin Moor in the 1860s. Many of the operations were small and only lasted into the first quarter of the 20th century. Parson's Park is one of only two pits that survived into the modern age and only closed in the last 10 years or so. The other is Stannon which will be seen later in the walk.

China clay is formed when granite starts to decompose, a process known as kaolinisation. The kaolin is separated from the rest of the granite by using high powered water jets which blast it from the rock. It is then piped as slurry to settling tanks before being dried and graded. It has many uses, not just in the making of porcelain. Most of the Cornish clay goes to the paper industry where it is used as filler in the paper itself and also in the production of the glossy coating found in many magazines.

What you can see of Parson's Park are the waste tips, banks of sand and rock that in time will hopefully become part of the surrounding moorland. Generally, for every ton of china clay extracted, there will be eight tons of waste. In the past these tips were high conical pyramids called skytips but health and safety regulations introduced in the 1970s saw the change to lower longer banks. You will see two of the old style tips at the Glynn Valley works later in the walk.

Berry Castle, St Neot:

Berry Castle is an Iron Age hillfort dating from sometime between 400 B.C and 49 A.D.

After the Bronze Age it is thought the climate up on Bodmin Moor became very inhospitable. People moved to lower ground where they were sheltered from the harsh weather. For many years the moors would have only been used for summer pasture or for defence. This hillfort is one such place. The views from atop the fort stretch away to the coast in the south, giving Iron Age man plenty of chances to spot any intruders.

Although much of the fort is man-made, natural rock formations to the north and south of the hilltop have been included in the construction. Inside the fort, detail is not very clear: stones lie scattered all over the place and although some may be the remains of hut circles, many more look as though they have always been there, unusual in a fort of this design.

The name Berry is said to come from the old English word "Byrig" meaning fort.

the north and the eastern side of **Parson's Park China Clay Works**, its white waste tips heading off into the distance. Over to the northeast is the old engine house of Wheal Northwood mine, now converted into a dwelling.

Here we leave the Two Valleys Walk and take the footpath that goes off to the left. This runs through bracken and boulders and is not very clear in places. Fingerposts have been placed along the way; keep an eye out for them. The path passes below **Berry Castle,** an Iron Age hillfort. Apart from the outer banks very little can be seen of this settlement, much of it overgrown like the surrounding hillside.

Contouring around to the left, follow the signposts through the bracken. After a while you will reach a wall on your left hand side. Follow it, passing a gateway with a stile leading into a field. Do not cross this stile however, as the path you must take continues onwards until the

wall, now just a collection of lumps of stone, runs out. Keep going in the same direction following the fence to another stile. Go over this and keeping the hedge on your right proceed to the road.

The public footpath carries straight on across the road and soon enters a field via a stile. Turn left and head downhill, keeping close to the hedge until it veers away to the left. At this point carry on down across this field and the next, towards the gate and onto the road. Take the lane opposite that leads gently downhill to Higher Newton Farm where an unsurfaced lane goes off to the left. This leads down to the village of **St Neot** where it joins the road again just behind the old primary school. Turn left. At the end of the road you arrive at a T-junction in the village. Here you can visit the pub, the church, the Holy Well or the Doorstep Green. If you have time to spare you may wish to walk a mile or so east of

St Neot Holy Well

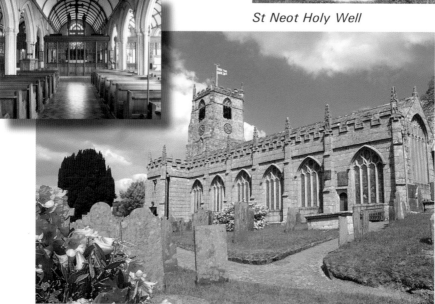

St Neot Church

Carnglaze Caverns

the village passing St Neot Pottery, to the Carnglaze Slate Caverns. This is an underground slate quarry that is open to the public with guided tours available. During the World War II the Navy used the cavern to store surplus rum here and nowadays "The Rum Store" is used to host underground music concerts. If you wish to visit the Doorstep Green, turn right at the junction, pass the Post Office, go over the bridge and take the first left. The green can then be reached by crossing the playing field and then the river to your left.

The Doorstep Green

St Neot:

Snuggled into its own little valley on the southern edge of the moor, the village of St Neot has plenty to offer the moorland traveller, be it spiritual, historical, musical or edible.

The saint after whom the village is named has origins open to argument. Could he have been a Celtic saint, also connected with the village of Menheniot east of Liskeard? Or is he the Saxon relative of King Alfred who left Glastonbury to seek solitude in Cornwall? The experts seem to have come to the conclusion

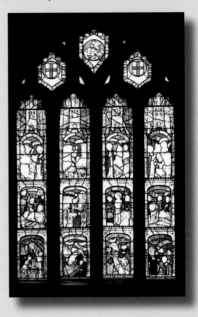

that St Neot is a combination of the two, and his story, told in wonderful detail on windows in the church, is well worth viewing.

It is not just the story of St Neot that adorns the church windows. Both the Creation and the legend of St George and the Dragon are represented amongst others and they are said to be some of the finest 16th century windows of their type in the whole of the UK.

Outside the church there are four ancient crosses brought here from various parts of the parish. Alongside them is a lantern cross, originally from St Kew on the northwest side of the moor. Above you, sticking out from the top of the tower, you should be able to see an oak branch. This is renewed every year on Oak Apple Day, 29th May, and dates back to the Civil War when the area supported the King. A copy of the King Charles letter sent to the people of Cornwall in 1643 can be found in the church.

Next door to the church is the London Inn, a popular watering hole and also handy for a spot of lunch. The name derives from when St Neot was on the main coaching route between London and Penzance. The inn would have been a welcome stop-off point. Nowadays the inn takes centre stage in the village voted best in England and Wales in 2004, an award it thoroughly deserves.

CARBURROW
TOR

WHITEWALLS

TOR
HOUSE

TREVEDDOE

WARLEGGAN

Day 2
St Neot to Bodmin
13 miles

TO MOUNT

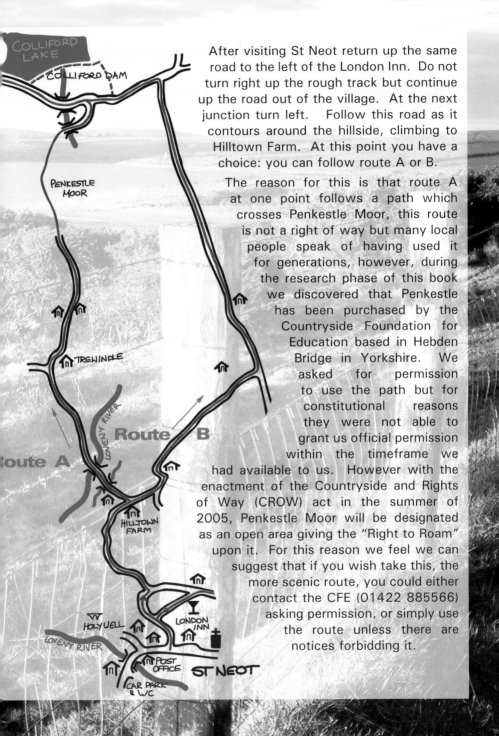

After visiting St Neot return up the same road to the left of the London Inn. Do not turn right up the rough track but continue up the road out of the village. At the next junction turn left. Follow this road as it contours around the hillside, climbing to Hilltown Farm. At this point you have a choice: you can follow route A or B.

The reason for this is that route A at one point follows a path which crosses Penkestle Moor, this route is not a right of way but many local people speak of having used it for generations, however, during the research phase of this book we discovered that Penkestle has been purchased by the Countryside Foundation for Education based in Hebden Bridge in Yorkshire. We asked for permission to use the path but for constitutional reasons they were not able to grant us official permission within the timeframe we had available to us. However with the enactment of the Countryside and Rights of Way (CROW) act in the summer of 2005, Penkestle Moor will be designated as an open area giving the "Right to Roam" upon it. For this reason we feel we can suggest that if you wish take this, the more scenic route, you could either contact the CFE (01422 885566) asking permission, or simply use the route unless there are notices forbidding it.

COLLIFORD LAKE

COLLIFORD DAM

PENKESTLE MOOR

TREWINDLE

LOVENY RIVER

Route B

Route A

HILLTOWN FARM

HOLY WELL

LOVENY RIVER

LONDON INN

POST OFFICE

ST NEOT

CAR PARK & WC

Colliford Lake

Route A

Just past the farm turn left again and drop down into the Loveny valley, crossing over two bridges and entering Trevenna Woods. The road follows the Loveny River (also known as the St Neot River) for a short while before climbing away from it, ignore the next left and carry on up the hill. After passing several small farmsteads and a large modern barn complex, the road comes to an end. A gate leads out on to Penkestle Moor; please make sure you close it after going through. Please keep as close to

the track as possible as it crosses the moor, staying close to the right hand side wall. Great views open up as you make your way along the track, especially of **Colliford Lake**, directly in front.

As the track descends, it curves around to the right and crosses the Loveny River via a bridge. The surface of the track improves and soon reaches the road running below the dam. (A diversion can be made here by turning right up the road a short distance to reach a permissive path that runs along the top of the dam.) Turning left; follow the road as it climbs out of the valley passing the car parks for those who wish to view the lake.

Route B

Ignore the left turn and carry on along the road to a T junction. Here turn left and continue along the road past Tremaddock Farm, with the wooded Loveny valley below you on your left. The road climbs gradually back towards Berry Down. When another T junction is reached turn left again. After crossing the lower slopes of Mutton Down the road straightens and proceeds for about a mile towards **Colliford Lake**. To your right are the abandoned china clay works at Parson's Park whilst beyond them is the rounded hill of Brown Gelly.

At the end of the road turn left and drop down below the dam, climbing the other side and passing the car parks for those who wish view the lake. *Route A rejoins at this point*.

At the end of the road turn right and continue along until you reach open moorland.

Once out onto the open moor and having passed the cattle grid, turn left along the lane to Warleggan and Mount. This drops down into a valley below **Carburrow Tor**, crosses a bridge and climbs up the other side. As the road begins to level out it turns slightly to the left and a track goes off on the right towards a farmhouse. Take this and follow it across two fields to Tor House. Here the public right of way goes left in front of the house and across the yard to a gate. Once through the gateway the footpath picks its way across the lower slopes of Carburrow Tor, an area littered with the remains of earlier settlements. The true path is not easy to follow amongst so much

Glynn Valley Clay Works

Colliford Lake:

During the 1970s arguments raged as to where to site a third reservoir on the Moor. Two sites were chosen, the Draynes valley or here above Colliford Downs. In the end this site was chosen and in 1984 the work was finished and the St Neot River dammed. It is now a brown trout fishery run by Southwest Lakes Trust with tickets available from Colliford Tavern, and an overwintering site for wildfowl.

Carburrow Tor:

Since "discovering" this tor whilst researching a walk in Warleggan parish a couple of years back, I have constantly been drawn back to it. It is not the most well known hill on Bodmin Moor by a long way, but it is surprising, that once you know where it is, you can see it from so many places.

The hill is covered in history, from the un-modernised farmstead at Tor House to the Bronze Age cairns that sit on top. The remains of a medieval long house can be found on the left, shortly after going through the gate at Tor House. Climbing up the hillside to the top you walk through a Bronze Age village full of hut circles. Judging by their size, the two cairns at the summit must have had great significance. Can it be a coincidence that the profile of the cairns on top of the hill replicates the profiles of Brown Willy and Roughtor: the highest points in Cornwall?

During WW2 the eastern one was dug into and used as a look out point for the local home guard.

Glynn Valley China Clay Works:

Opened in 1875 and owned, like many of the clay works on Bodmin Moor, by Frank Parkyn. The valley had earlier been used for shallow mining operations, evidence of which can still be seen on the eastern side. The clay produced here was never of any great quality and the site was worked on and off until the mid 1900s. There is still much to be seen at Glynn for anyone interested in industrial history and a footpath runs through the centre of the site. The moorland to the west of the works is a danger area when firing is taking place on the Fore Downs range, hence the occasional red flag hoisted on the nearby tip.

Wheal Whisper:

Tin was being mined in this valley at the start of the 1700s and possibly long before. A great open cast pit still exists up river in the woods but is not accessible to the public. The lovely name, Wheal Whisper, is said to be linked to the fact that even in later years most of the machinery at the mine was driven by waterwheels, the area being too remote to make it cost effective to bring coal from the coast to fuel steam driven engines. The ruined building in the valley is the former miners' dry and workshop, a dry being where they could change after a hard day's work.

Warleggan:

The small village of Warleggan sits hidden from the masses, rarely visited except by those seeking out the church and the story of its former parson. He was the Rev Densham and it was Daphne du Maurier's version of his time in the village that draws people there. He was, if we

history but by keeping close to the wall on your left another gate should soon be found at Whitewalls.

Go through the gate and down beside the house. The track eventually joins the road via a cattle grid. Turn left and climb the road towards Warleggan Down. When the brow of the hill is reached it is worth turning round and looking down the valley to the left of Carburrow Tor. The conical sky tips of the **Glynn Valley Clay Works** mark the site of late 19th century china clay workings last used in the 1940s.

After crossing another cattle grid turn right down the farm track towards Treveddoe (over yet another grid). The farmhouse here

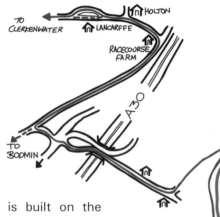

is built on the site of an old manor house that was destroyed by fire. The route of the official footpath here is a little unclear but with the help of the owners we suggest the following: During the summer, when the weather is dry and there are no cattle in the field, turn left as you arrive at the farmyard, pass around

the buildings keeping them on your right. As you go through one field and into the next, at the end of the buildings you will see a gate on your right and the main house as well. Turn left here, going down the hill to rejoin the official path in the bottom of the valley near a disused building. During the winter, when the ground is likely to be wet and there will be cattle in the field, we would advise sticking entirely to the official route which is: Upon arriving at the farmyard, bear left immediately through a gate and head for the stone garden wall in front. Follow the path around to the left in front of the wall, descending a few yards to another gate, then carry on down the hill through two more gateways until you reach the valley bottom and a disused building.

Signs tell you to keep clear of the building, once part of the **Wheal Whisper** mining complex (also known as Treveddoe) further up the valley. The river to the right is the Bedalder or **Warleggan** River that in a few miles will join the Fowey River in the Glynn Valley (not to be confused with the Glynn Valley to the north). From here the path follows the river, passing a landscaped quarry on the left and another chimney on the right before a gate leads into the woods.

The track through the woods comes out on the road that leads up to Warleggan. Here turn right and head down to Wooda Bridge. Cross over the bridge and follow the road as it winds uphill onto open moorland. As it levels out, it once again becomes enclosed, picking

Inscribed Stones

its way between the fields to the village of Mount.

At the crossroads in the village turn right and head back out towards the open moor. Pass Mount Pleasant Farm on the right, before turning left down the next lane. This quiet country lane will now be followed for the next mile or so until you reach Little Downs. About half way along, at a crossroads, two stones are passed, standing high on the right hand side bank. They have Latin inscriptions on them, now well eroded, and are thought to date from the 10th century.

On reaching Little Downs follow the

believe her words, an eccentric man who fell out with all his parishioners, to the point that he erected cardboard effigies in the church just to have someone to preach to. The reasons for his falling out with the parishioners are many, but was he eccentric or just out of place amongst people not used to outsiders? After speaking to people in the village who remember hearing about him from relatives, it seems he may not have been quite as "strange" as du Maurier made out. Putting aside the story of the Rev Densham, the church is a pleasant place to visit and tends to be open most of the time.

Cardinham Castle:

All that can be seen of this grand sounding site is a grassy bank in a field. Considering it had been abandoned by the 14th century perhaps we should not be surprised. It was built in Norman times by Richard Fitz-Turold, the first Lord of Cardinham and one wonders why he chose this site tucked away up a valley on the edge of the moor.

Cardinham Woods:

One of the most popular areas for outdoor recreation in East Cornwall, you will be very lucky if you manage to get through the woods without meeting a jogger, cyclist, horse rider or just another walker. The centre of the woods is the Ladyvale Bridge, situated at a site near to where there was, in the 12th century, a

Ladyvale Bridge, Cardinham Woods

chapel. Nothing now remains except for the old clapper bridge, preserved from 21st century "pilgrims" by fencing.

There are over 10 miles of signposted trails in the woods plus many more tracks and paths that lead off into the quiet dark depths. The path we follow passes the Wheal Glynn Trail which leads up to the ruin of a mine where galena or silver lead was mined in the 1800s. Once past Ladyvale, our route climbs up a

road around to the right with the green on your left. Cross the road and go down the lane opposite. On your right you will see an old road sign confirming that there is a bridleway ¾ of a mile further on. The road turns to the left in front of a cottage and then passes the remains of **Cardinham Castle** on the right. Continue along to Castle Farm where the aforementioned bridleway turns right and downhill, opposite the farmhouse going beside a pond and to the left of an old barn. The reason for the pond can be seen to your right, if you have sharp eyes, just as you pass the barn.

Go through the gate beyond the barn and keep to the hedge high up on the right. The path climbs above the valley with good views over to the village of Cardinham, before descending steeply to a stone bridge over a stream. Once over, follow the narrow sunken pathway as it climbs to the road (the last section goes

Castle Farm Water Wheel

through someone's garden, please pass through quickly and quietly).

Unless you wish to visit the church, turn left and follow the road as it descends to a bridge over the stream known as Cardinham Water. The road then climbs gently before branching off to the right and following the valley and the beech trees of Parsonage Wood to Milltown. Here turn left just before Lang's Mill and continue along the lane until the very end. Here you will find the entrance to **Cardinham Woods**, a simple barrier preventing vehicle access. Go past the barrier and up onto a wide forestry track. Turn right.

With the stream on your right, follow the track through the trees until you reach a large junction of tracks at Ladyvale Bridge. Turn right going over the stream and then go round to the left crossing another stream. Once over this second stream immediately turn right and follow the track up the left hand side of the valley. Staying on this side of the valley you will eventually come to the end of the track where a path carries on at the same level into woodland. This path is only short and soon a stile is reached on the right leading into a field. Go over this and follow the bottom edge of the field to the far end where another stile can be found beside a gate.

Crossing the stile, an old track is to be found, *Bugle* *flowers May to July* now used mainly by rabbits. Turn left and climb between the well burrowed banks eventually coming out into a field. Keeping to the left hand side of the field, continue to the corner where two gateways can be found. The right hand one leads onto a continuation of the old track and will bring you out at Callybarrett cottage where you turn right onto a lane. Follow this lane as it passes Callybarrett Farm and a track to Racecourse Farm, before running adjacent to the slip road off the **A30** which you will soon pass over. The next road you will come to is the A389, a busy road but much quieter than the A30. Find a safe place to cross; you need to go down the road opposite, signposted Helland.

If you wish to break your journey to visit **Bodmin**, adding a further 3 miles to the route, then you should keep left at the turning to Helland and follow the Old Callywith Road down into Bodmin. As you approach the church, take the turning to your right as the road bends to the left and descend to a T-junction. By turning left, then right at the mini roundabout you are soon in Bodmin town centre. However, to rejoin the Copper Trail, turn right at the T-junction and, after passing a car showroom on your right and a pelican crossing, take a turning on your right signposted to the Camel Trail cycle route. Continue on this road past the Fire station and Bodmin Gaol, to the Camel Trail. Follow the trail and signposts for Poley's Bridge.

valley that has been cleared of many trees in recent years; this allows other plants to thrive, including rosebay willow herb and bluebells.

On quiet days you may be lucky and spot a deer or two. You should have no problem spotting squirrels, and the sight of a buzzard soaring overhead is a common occurrence. However if you spot an otter or a dormouse make sure you tell someone; they are known to be active in the woods but sightings are rare.

A30:

The main trunk road down through the county, the A30 is a blessing for many travellers but creates a huge barrier for the walker on Bodmin Moor. Between Bodmin and Five Lanes there are only two other places where it is safe to cross, both the far side of Bolventor. The route it follows is ancient, leaving the old Cornish capital of Launceston and running across the high moor to Bodmin. Along the way crosses were erected in the 10th and 11th centuries to guide people and also to give them somewhere to pray for safe passage.

In the middle of the moor, Jamaica Inn became the stopping off point for coaches and somewhere to refresh the horses. Coaches still stop, but now it serves to refresh tourists, hungry for the myth created by Daphne du Maurier in her novel of the same name.

Racecourse Farm:

Bodmin Racecourse was first mentioned in 1642 when Cavalier troops gathered there at the start of the Civil War. It was used as a racecourse until 1790 when a dispute between local gentry caused it to be closed down. It opened again in 1806, but by 1842 it had closed for good and in 1876 the Cornwall Golf Club took over the area. The golf course survived until World War II when the land was ploughed up in order to feed the country. It is thought the old Racecourse Farm building was once the Racecourse Inn, where horses had to be taken one day prior to the races.

Clerkenwater:

Towards the end of the 1700s a tan house was set up in this quiet valley just north of Bodmin. It didn't last long and soon a small woollen mill had taken its place. After a fire had destroyed almost all of the buildings in 1800 the mill was rebuilt on a slightly grander scale and went on to produce blankets, serge and cloth for sailors.

Bodmin:

The county town of Cornwall for many years, Bodmin is still a bustling shopping centre despite the main county offices and court being moved to Truro. The Tourist Information Centre and museum can be found in the central square and the old County Gaol can be visited at the top end of the Camel Trail. Lovers of steam can ride on restored trains on two lines to the south of the town whilst those with an interest in military matters can visit the Infantry Museum opposite the station.

Day 3
Bodmin to St Breward
10 miles

TO PEND

BUSLAND INN

BLISLAND

LAVETHAN

W·C

P·C

Wood-Sorrel
flowers April to June,
flowers and
leaves close
up at night

CAMEL·TRAIL

HELLANDBRIDGE

RIVER CAMEL

CAMEL TRAIL

FROM BODMIN

FROM RACECOURSE FARM

CLERKENWATER HOUSE

Alternatively, if you did not visit Bodmin, take the Helland road which branches off to the right and follows the route of the old A30 as it climbs alongside the new A30. As you reach the brow of the hill you find the other half of **Racecourse Farm** on the left hand side. Turn left and follow the road that goes between the buildings past The Royal Links.

At the next group of buildings, Holten, take the left hand fork. This goes towards Lancarffe. Officially the footpath goes straight on through the complex of buildings but it is just as easy to veer to the right at the start of the drive and follow the track around the barns.

This lane now continues for some distance between the fields towards **Clerkenwater**. It eventually narrows as it enters woodland. Soon you will reach a house. Pass by to the right and join the drive which takes you down to the road. Turn right over the bridge then left down a track beside the Old Laundry Cottage. This passes the ruins of the old woollen mill before coming to a ford over the river - don't worry, there is a good footbridge as well. The track then climbs through the woods to Copshorn Farm where it curves around to the left and becomes surfaced.

A little further on a lane goes off to the right through a gate, with just enough room to squeeze through between gate and hedge. Across the fields on the left, the monument on the hill above **Bodmin** can be seen; the town itself is hidden in the valley below. At the next gate, a stile makes life easier and the track then runs around the top edge of an open field to another gate into East Wood. Once in the woods the footpath turns left and runs downhill, crossing other paths to regain the forestry track at a lower level. Carry on down until you reach the **Camel Trail** then turn right and follow the former railway line for about 4 miles. The first road crossing you will come to is at Helland Bridge, after which you will meet the road again at Shell Woods. Not far after this you will reach Tresarrett and a signpost which has Pollpons written on it. Leave the trail here and turn right then right again. Follow the road past the houses and, at the next junction, follow the road round to the left signposted Cardinham and Launceston. The climb may come as a shock after the flat of the Camel Trail but it does not last long. At the second gate on the left take the footpath going off up steps.

As you enter the field, the house ahead of you on the other side of the

Camel Trail in its Former Glory....

valley is **Lavethan**. Descend the field to the bottom left hand corner where you enter Lavethan Woods, now owned by The Woodland Trust. The path descends to the right, passing a large badger sett before reaching a short ladder that takes you down into the field. It is best to go down this ladder backwards. Once in the field proceed across it towards a gate to your right. Do not go through this gate but walk a little further upstream to where a single piece of granite spans the river. Cross this with care and head up the field to firm ground. The footpath goes off to the right, crossing to a gateway where it joins a surfaced track that contours up the side of the hill. At the top of the hill a gate is reached and **Blisland Church** appears in front of you. Head towards it.

....and now

After visiting the church, exit by the main gate out on to **Blisland** village green, one of very few in Cornwall. The route out of the village is ahead of you in the top right hand corner of the green, but take some time to explore the village a little before heading onwards.

At the top of the green is a crossroads. Take the turning going north with no direction on the signpost (don't take the cycle route). This leads along a lane to another crossroads where you go straight ahead towards Pendrift - a hamlet which is a mixture of renovated barns, old cottages and unsightly rubbish. Head straight through to a gate leading into a short stretch of muddy track. This takes you into a field where you need to keep to the right hand side hedge; go through another gateway and as it descends, you eventually reach a wooden stile. Once over the stile a large open area stretches out below you. Away to the right can be seen the edge of De Lank granite quarry whilst the De Lank River may be heard but not seen. Follow the path as it descends to the open area below. When you reach a solitary hawthorn tree, turn to the right to go under the overhead cables. The path now proceeds across the gorse and bracken covered plain towards the De Lank gorge (in winter this path can be wet underfoot). The steep wooded hillside gets closer on the right hand side all the time. Just as you start to feel you are going to end up entering the woods, the path climbs amongst boulders and the sound of running water increases.

The source of the water is soon found as you enter a wonderful sylvan setting. Here, trees grow out of lichen covered rocks, and the De Lank River rushes down through them in an effort to escape the high moor and seek out the gentle pastures below. In my view this is a far more impressive setting than Golitha Falls and yet the chances of meeting anyone are pretty slim. When you finally tire of the place, take the footbridge over the river and follow the path as it turns left to run down the opposite bank. You will find yourself walking alongside some large pipes and soon come to a disused building. Do not attempt to go inside. This is the former hydro-electric generating station for the De Lank quarries, installed in 1927. The path now climbs with views opening out to the west, whilst a spoil tip of granite is all that can be seen of the large workings beyond the hill to the right. As the path levels out, it zig-zags, and for a very short stretch you follow the course of the tramway that used to run from the quarry down to the railway line at Wenford.

After passing a house on your right you will reach the quarry road. This enters the workings via a large

De Lank River

The Camel Trail and the River Camel:

This popular recreational trail was created in the 1980s after the railway line that ran from Bodmin to Wenford china clay dries, closed. It is the quieter of the two arms of the Camel Trail, the other one running from Bodmin to Padstow via Wadebridge.

The original railway line was created in 1834, one of the first in the world. It was never intended for passengers and for most of its life served the china clay and granite industries of the St Breward area. Nowadays it provides many miles of off road walking, cycling or horse riding on level ground.

The river itself winds along beside the trail on its way to the sea. It is the only Cornish river of any size to join the Atlantic via the north coast and forms the western boundary of the moor.

It is renowned for its fishing (several fishermen's paths lead from the trail but they are not for public access). The river is also a popular haunt for otters. These shy creatures have made a successful comeback in recent years and can now be found on nearly every river in Cornwall.

Lavethan:

The present house at Lavethan dates from the 16th century although there have been many alterations over the years. There was a house here as early as 1475, owned by the Kempe family until 1654 when it was sold to Christopher Walker. Since then it has passed through various families, either by death or marriage to the present owner James Morshead Glencross.

The original features of the house were used to great advantage during the filming of the BBC drama, Poldark and more recently Amy Foster.

The woodland opposite the house now belongs to the Woodland Trust but was once part of the Lavethan estate. The majority of the trees are oak which in the past would have been coppiced for charcoal, building and firewood. Nowadays there are many other types of trees to be found on the north-facing hillside, including larch and Douglas fir, many of which will be removed as part of the trust's management plan to return the woods to their natural state.

Blisland Church:

Most of the churches that you will visit along the route are typical solidly built structures with cold granite interiors, devoid of decoration apart from the odd stained glass window. From the outside Blisland looks very much the same, but once inside, prepare to be amazed. Here on the edge of Bodmin Moor you will find yourself taken back 500 years to before the reformation when churches were full of colour. Not that the décor in Blisland is 500 years old: the Rood screen that takes your breath away is only just over a hundred years old.

The church is dedicated to St Pratt although this is believed to be a derivation of St Protus, who with his brother St Hyacinth were the saints connected to the church since the middle ages. Little is known about them except that they were Roman martyrs and that Blisland remains the only church in the UK to be dedicated to them.

A slate memorial to the Kempe family who owned Lavethan can be found in the Lady Chapel. It is crudely carved, the carver having forgotten to put the word "that" into the original line and having had to add it later.

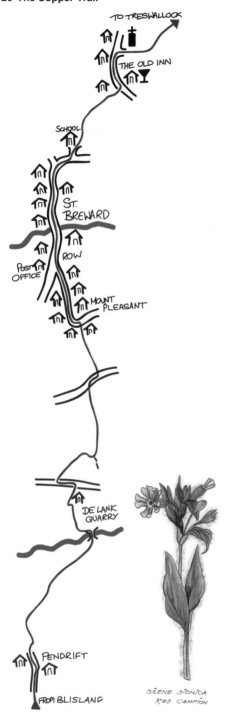

TO TRESWALLOCK

THE OLD INN

SCHOOL

ST. BREWARD

ROW

POST OFFICE

MOUNT PLEASANT

DE LANK QUARRY

PENDRIFT

FROM BLISLAND

SILENE DIOINCA
RED CAMPION

cutting created after the tramway was abandoned in the 1940s. Although there is a well used gate opposite, the official route of the footpath from here actually enters the field further down the lane to your left. A metal gate gives access to the field from where the path diagonally heads back up towards the top edge. Here the OS map shows the footpath continuing along the edge of the field before joining up with another path coming in on the right. This now seems to have been changed and a stile leads over the fence and climbs between gorse and rocks to the edge of the **De Lank Quarry**. Here it turns left (by turning right for a short while you will get good views down into

the quarry) and follows the old boundary wall through rough pasture to a combination of stone steps and a wooden stile into fields.

Follow the fence as it passes an obsolete stone stile and continue in the same direction through two more fields before reaching the road. Be careful descending the last stile onto the road if it is wet. Turn right up the road a short distance before turning left up and over another granite stile and through a modern gate. You are now in a field which goes by the strange name of Taggarts Platt. Follow the path as it leads across the open area before it narrows between dry stone walls leading to a gate and a tarmac path to the road.

You are now at the southern end of the group of communities that make up the village of **St Breward**, this area being known as Mount Pleasant. Turn left here and follow the road as it runs between old cottages and modern houses towards the centre of the village. This is reached at Row where both the Post Office and the general stores can be found, as well as the main road which must now be joined as you turn right. Go past the Methodist Church and down the road crossing the village stream. The road now climbs and leaves yet another part of the village behind. When you reach the lane to the school on the left, go down it and follow the footpath as it goes beside the school and winds between the fields to a farmyard. When you arrive, go straight across the yard and out on to the road opposite **The Old Inn**.

Blisland:

Despite the fact that Blisland has a wonderful church and some fine old buildings arranged around a village green, it is for the pub that many people visit the village. The Blisland Inn has over the last few years, been creating something of a name for itself. This culminated in 2001 when it was named National Pub of the Year by CAMRA (Campaign for Real Ale). As well as always having a good selection of real ales on sale, the landlord Gary Marshall also stocks local cider and serves "hearty home made food" (Good Pub Guide 2004), Just what you need for a good walk!

De Lank Quarry:

The precise date when granite was first quarried here at De Lank is not known, but is thought to be about the mid 1800s. Things developed quickly, no doubt aided by the rail links the quarry had to the coast at Padstow and Fowey. In the early 1880s the quarry was given the contract to supply stone for the new Eddystone Lighthouse and a part of the quarry is still named after this relatively local job. Further afield many of London's landmarks contain De Lank granite: Blackfriars, Putney and Tower Bridge, The Thames Embankment, New Scotland Yard, The Cenotaph and the Karl Marx memorial in Highgate cemetery to name but a few. Even as far away as India, cornish stone found a use; the docks at Bombay (now Mumbai) were built from De Lank granite.

Nowadays De Lank is the only large stone quarry still operating on the moor and it is from here that in early 2005 a lump of granite weighing approximately 180 tons was taken. This is to be carved into a giant seed to take centre stage at the Eden Project near St Austell.

St Breward:

This long drawn out village is in fact made up of four or five settlements from Limehead in the south to the Churchtown at the top end. It is a mixture of old granite cottages and modern bungalows, many enjoying the wonderful views that come with living on an escarpment. The centre of the village is at Row where you will find the Post Office and village shop, which also has a small tourist information display tucked away in the right hand corner at the back.

There are public toilets behind the post office.

The Old Inn:

No one knows how old the Old Inn is. The earliest mention of it only takes us back as far as 1806, but it is claimed to date from the 11th Century. It has been said that if this building is the Old Inn, then there must have been a more recent drinking establishment in the village. There are records of alehouses opening up in the mid 1800s but no other Inns, the difference being, that an alehouse would only sell ale, whilst an Inn sold wine and spirits and should also be able to provide food and accommodation.

These days the Inn is a welcome stop for those walking on this side of the moor, the huge fireplace being most welcome after battling against a south-westerly whilst coming back from Brown Willy. Like the Blisland Inn, the Old Inn also comes highly recommended by the Good Pub Guide 2004.

Day 4
St Breward
to Camelford
6 miles

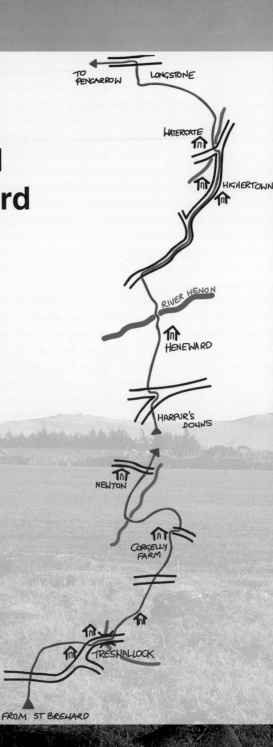

TO PENCARROW

LONGSTONE

WATERGATE

HIGHERTOWN

RIVER HENON

HENEWARD

HARPUR'S DOWNS

NEWTON

CORGELLY FARM

TRESHALLOCK

FROM ST BREWARD

Next door to the The Old Inn is **St Breward Church**. Turn right along the lane running in front of it. Follow this for a short distance before turning left over a stone stile into a field. The route from here continues diagonally across six fields, each with a stone stile to negotiate. Exiting the last field brings you to a road. Cross this and go over another stile. From now on many of the stiles have wooden bars that can be lifted to make access easier. From experience all of them stayed up unattended whilst I climbed over, but I would always check first.

Once over the hedge, head towards the mound of stones with the water tank on top. The footpath goes to the left of this and over the wall. If you are walking this route after heavy rain it may provide you with a wet foot. My advice is to climb up onto the wall and follow it towards the farm for a short distance until the ground below you to the left looks solid. The footpath carries on across the field to join a track that runs down to the left of Treswallock Farm and in front of Treswallock Cottage. From here join the road for a short distance as it descends to cross a low bridge, only noticeable if the stream is running full under it. Once over the bridge a stile leads over the hedge on the left.

The footpath snakes through a meadow, where groups of trees have been fenced off for protection. It then passes into another field that runs behind Mellon Farm for a few yards before going through a gateway on the right. Once in this third field turn left and head for the top right corner. Another long narrow field must be walked across before

Orchis mascula
EARLY PURPLE ORCHID

At Rest

a road is once again reached. Cross the road and over another stile where there is a nice view of Alex Tor on your right. Head across the field towards the pine trees, picking up a wall on your right, half way across. Follow this to the right hand metal gate towards the farmyard.

The footpath seems to have been diverted from the route marked on the OS map. Instead of going left down through Corgelly Farm you are directed right up the lane a short distance to where steps and a stile lead into a very muddy field. My advice here is to take a large arc out around the barn keeping as far left as you can but avoiding the churned up mud made by the cattle. The path, once past the barn, descends into the valley. The official route should go down the sunken lane beside the field, but this is very overgrown and not passable; just keep as close to it as you can.

At the bottom of the field you will find a footbridge over the stream. Be careful if this is wet, as the wood can be very slippery and the mud very deep. Once over the stream

Harpur's Down looking towards Roughtor

go straight ahead through a gap in the hedge and then turn right along the bottom of the field. This takes you below Newton to a stile (again slippery when wet) leading down into an old lane. On the other side of the lane, granite steps lead you to a stile and into a small plantation. Make your way through the trees, avoiding the low branches, to yet another stile. From this point the path follows the bottom of the fields as it runs along the edge of a marshy valley. **Roughtor and Brown Willy** can both be viewed ahead to the right along with the man made hill of **Stannon China Clay Works.**

The last stile is a short distance up from the bottom of the field and leads out onto open moorland on Harpurs Down. Climb gently towards the road, which is hidden until you reach it. Turn right along it towards a gateway. Several stones are passed on the left at the junction; they are not thought to be part of an ancient monument but sitting here in the shadow of Roughtor they could very well be. Cross another road here and go through the two gateways using the stiles provided. Follow the track towards Heneward, branching off to the left just before the house is reached. Follow the path as it turns right through a gap and descends diagonally towards the trees and the telegraph pole. A small, well hidden stile is negotiated before reaching the bottom of the valley and a footbridge over the **Henon River**.

You are now in the parish of Advent. The footpath turns right after crossing the bridge and winds

St Breward Church:

Said to be the highest church in Cornwall (in altitude not height), St Breward Church is virtually the last building in the village. Parts of the chancel date back to Norman times but much of what can be seen nowadays is the result of restoration work done in the mid 1800s. This was done under the supervision of JP St Aubyn, who also worked on many other churches in Cornwall around the same time. His "work" was heavily criticised by the poet Sir John Betjeman who believed he had destroyed more than he had saved.

Roughtor and Brown Willy:

These two "hills" dominate much of the northern moor and can be seen from many places along the walk. Brown Willy is the higher of the two at 1375ft (420 meters), the highest point in Cornwall. Roughtor stands about 60 ft lower, but often looks the more impressive of the two, with its rugged crest of granite sheltering the remains of the medieval chapel dedicated to St Michael. It is pronounced row tor as in cow, and is in the hands of the National Trust. A good way to access it is via the car park at the end of the road from Tregoodwell.

Brown Willy is not so easy to get to, although continuing on from Roughtor is most people's choice. Another way is to walk from Candra (east of St Breward) out past King Arthur's Hall and around Garrow Tor. From here a permissive footpath leads up the spine of the hill to the top.

Stannon China Clay Works:

Like Parson's Park above St Neot, Stannon only closed down a few years ago. Some reworking of the waste tips has taken place since, but they still dominate this part of the walk. Work started here in the 1870s at about the same time as work started at Heneward, just down the valley. Little remains at Heneward apart from a chimney and some very overgrown tanks, whilst here at Stannon after a slow start, things took off in the early 20th century. By 1910 50,000 tons of clay a year were flowing down pipes to Wenford at the end of the railway line where a dry was built at Poley's Bridge. Over the years, ownership of the works has changed on a regular basis, but the end of production came when the French company Imerys took over in the 1990s, giving the poor quality of the clay as a reason to close the works down.

Henon River:

Much of the water that fuels the Henon River these days, flows from within the Stannon Clay works. The rest of it has its source amongst the Crowdy marsh and the reservoir of the same name. As rivers go, it is never much more than a stream, and only a mile from our crossing point, it joins the Camel to continue its serpentine route to the sea at Padstow. Its main claim to fame is that it is the river that flows through the valley containing the Devil's Jump, two outcrops of rock facing each other across the valley.

through the woodland to some steps up into the fields. Once again, after heavy rain, you may find this area boggy. Climb the steps and keep to the left of the hedge that runs up the hillside. This will bring you to a long abandoned group of enclosures marked only by low walls topped by trees. Walk through and carry on up the hill to where a stile in the top right hand side of the field leads out onto a road. Turn right.

The road climbs gently upwards passing the entrance to Furhouse and on past Widewalls before arriving at the appropriately named Highertown. Here a little Methodist

A Tedder

chapel can be found still serving the community that once would have been made up of workers at the nearby Stannon China Clay Works across the valley. Descending the hill you will reach Watergate. Turn left over the stream and take the footpath on the right. This leads to a pleasant stretch of walking beside the moorland stream. Passing another abandoned settlement on the left and by keeping close to the stream, you arrive at two stiles. Go over these and once in the next field the path splits. Our route is diagonally and up to the left, climbing to the far corner of the field where a gate leads into another field. Stick to the field edge and you will reach another gate with a stile. Once over this you join a track.

You will not have failed to notice the standing stone in the centre of the field. After a while a stile leads off the track and you can make your

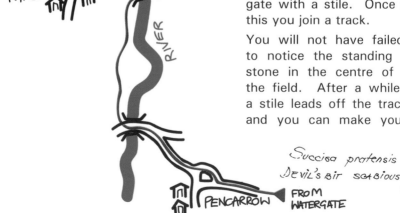

Succisa pratensis
DEViL's Bir scaBious
FROM
WATERGATE

Longstone

way towards it. The "Longstone" is an ancient monument that is thought to have originally been part of a larger structure. As with many other standing stones it is positioned on high ground, here giving far reaching views to the southwest. Leave the stone and carry on across the field to the left hand corner. Several other large stones lie in the grass. Were they once connected to the Longstone or just field clearance?

A wooden, then a granite stile lead onto the road. Here you turn left with good views down to the coast ahead of you. We must now follow this road as it descends through the hamlet of Pencarrow to Fenteroon Bridge. Here we meet the **River Camel** once again. Steps lead down onto the water meadow on the far side of the bridge to the right and from here a path is easy to follow as it runs beside the river all the way to **Camelford**. The footpath leaves the river after crossing a couple of bridges and climbs up some steps and under an arch to emerge on the main road through the town. Turn right and go down the hill passing the Darlington Arms, the Town Hall and the varied assortment of shops.

Camelford:

The little town lies just off the northwest edge of the moor and owes its existence to the fact that it was an important crossing point of the River Camel on the old road that ran from the west up to Exeter and beyond.

Today the main road, the A39, still brings traffic through the heart of the town and over the bridge which many years ago replaced the Camel ford. There is a good selection of shops and places to eat and stay.

North Cornwall Museum

For more help on accommodation the Tourist Information Centre is situated at the western end of the town in the same building as the museum, and is well worth a visit.

Day 5
Camelford to Five Lanes
10½ miles

At the bottom of the hill the Camel is crossed again where once the "camel ford" existed. Carry on up the road passing St Thomas's Church on the left and a little further up the old Bible Christian Chapel. Take the next turning on the right which is a one way road and leads through to the hamlet of Tregoodwell, now almost part of Camelford.

Reaching the "main" road, continue in the same direction dropping down to a bridge, before climbing up the long hill towards the open moor. This road eventually finishes at a car park used by people wanting to access Roughtor, but unless that is one of your quests, you should turn left at the top of the hill. This road follows a ridge going past the Lowermoor water treatment works. This waterworks became infamous in 1988 when 20 tons of aluminium sulphate were accidentally tipped into the local water supply. A little further along, Crowdy Reservoir is passed on the right before the road enters Davidstow Woods and the edge of the abandoned **Davidstow Airfield**.

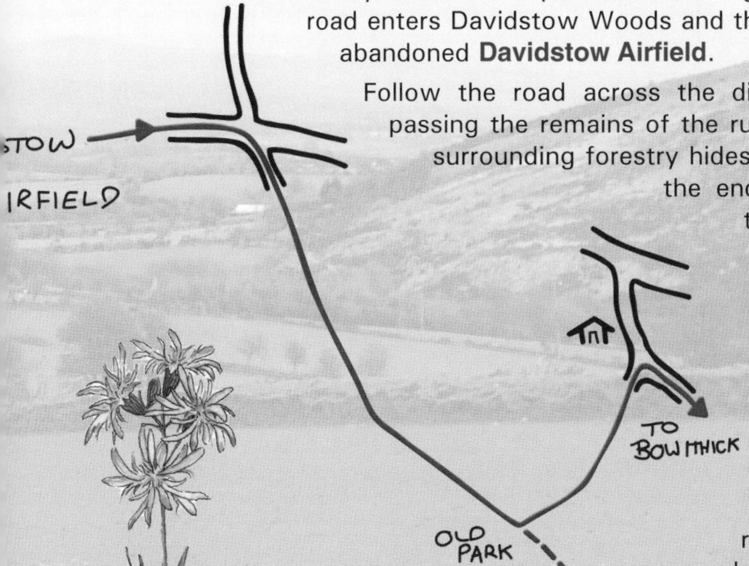

Follow the road across the disused airfield passing the remains of the runways. The surrounding forestry hides much, but at the end of the road turn right and head out along the road that crosses the main part of the airfield. The control tower sits back from the road on the far left, but other buildings can be passed at close quarters before a track is reached opposite the turning to Davidstow village. Walking

STOW

IRFIELD

TO BOWITHICK

OLD PARK

LYCHNIS FLOS-CUCULI
RAGGED ROBIN

along this track Crowdy Reservoir can now be seen over to the right, whilst in front of you the mass of Brown Willy looms. Go through the gate and carry on along the track, the surface of which soon degenerates as you get closer to Old Park. The buildings here are now

Brown Willy

the domain of the cattle and sheep that roam the moor and after rain this whole area can be a quagmire.

Just past the buildings, the path branches off to the left but it may be worth walking a little further on to take in the view. To the east the hills of Buttern and Carne sit guarding the moor from the north. To the south the featureless valley is home to

Bowithick Bridge

the source of the River Fowey, a boggy inhospitable area best left to the animals. Closer still, the remains of Roughtor Consuls mine are visible as mounds and dips in the neighbouring fields.

Return to Old Park and head towards the gate now on your right. Go through it and follow the tractor tracks as they head down the wide enclosure. After going through another gate the tracks multiply but still carry on in the same direction, eventually bringing you out onto the road at New Park. Here turn right and follow the road, which soon starts to descend gently towards the hamlet of Bowithick. The nearer you get, the deeper into the hillside the lane sinks until the banks on both sides tower above you. Once

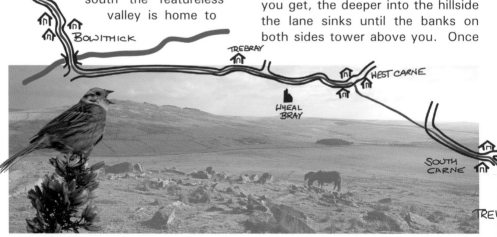

FROM DAVIDSTOW

BOWITHICK

TREBRAY

WHEAL BRAY

WEST CARNE

SOUTH CARNE

TREW

through the hamlet you regain the moor with **Bray Down** straight ahead of you. Cross over two fords (there are footbridges) and continue along the road as it turns to the left and contours along the base of the hill. Two landscapes contrast on either side of the road. To your right the hillside is covered in gorse and rock, whilst to your left are lush green fields. It is only when you see the rocks that make up the dividing walls of the fields a little further on, that you realise that the same rugged countryside once spread either side of the valley.

The road suddenly plunges down through the rocks to Trebray Farm where road and farm sometimes become one. A little further on it again descends to cross a stream near the former **Wheal Bray**, before a steep hill has to be climbed leading

Davidstow Airfield:

Opened in October 1942 to serve both the RAF and USAF, Davidstow airfield was blighted by the fact that it was often blanketed in fog or mist. Despite that, the USAF flew Flying Fortresses and Liberators from here and the RAF operated successful air sea rescue duties throughout the war.

At the end of the war it was decided to close down the airfield and it was left to the sheep and cattle to once again reclaim the moor. That is the scene today, although forestry has started to encroach on the southern edge, but that is not the whole story. In 1952 Cornwall Motor Racing Ltd was formed with the idea of creating a race track out of the old runways. This was done and several races took place over the next 3 years. Amongst them were three Formula One races including the first one at which a Lotus was raced. But once again it was weather that ruled the day, that and insurance costs.

Davidstow remains one of the least known Formula One tracks. Its airfield buildings now stand gaunt against the skyline and it is the Davidstow Creamery that takes the name forward, the cheese produced there being found all over the country.

Bray Down and Wheal Bray:

Standing at over 1000ft on the northeast corner of the moor, Bray Down offers fantastic views for anyone who endeavours to climb up its boulder strewn sides. This is one of the wildest parts of the moor, a ring of featureless hills stretching away towards the A30, below them marshes that have no mercy. It was out here, miles from anywhere, that an Italian POW camp was set up during the war. Elsewhere, man has made his mark with burial cairns on top of the hill and an Iron Age settlement on its northern flank.

Wheal Bray, which sits in the valley on the eastern side, was a copper mine in the mid 1800s. It closed down without making a profit but nearly reopened again in the 1950s when uranium was discovered on the waste tips. Although extensive trials were carried out, full scale work never got off the ground and the mine was left to fade into the hillside.

to West Carne. This little hamlet is very attractive and a plaque on the wall of one of the buildings gives recognition for conservation work done in recent years. The footpath leads off through a modern gate on the right, just as the road bends to the left. The path runs along the back of a private garden and over a set of steps into a field, where it runs along the bottom edge to an even taller set of steps and a stile. Once over these, cross the next field towards the top far right corner where more traditional stone steps lead over the wall beside a creep. Another couple of fields have to be crossed by keeping just to the right of the small barn and following the hedge to the road. Once on the road go straight ahead.

After the manicured lawns and converted barns of West Carne, South Carne will bring you back down to earth. This is still very much a working farm, and although you are on a public road, it is one very rarely used by any traffic except for farm traffic. A track leads off on the right just after passing the farmhouse. It is a nice wide track lined by trees but can be wet after rain. Just as the track appears to near its end, the hedge stops, and on the left there are two gates. Go through the second and follow the "tractor" track down through the field and across a stream. A stile at the end of the field leads into an old enclosed lane for a short distance before a footbridge and stile lead into another field. Walk to the top left of this field and cross into a larger field. Here the top right hand side hedge should be followed ignoring the first opening on the

Altarnun Bridge

Altarnun:

Famed for its church and Holy well, the pretty village of Altarnun sits just off the route of the walk. It is worth a detour if time allows and has the added bonus of a general store and post office.

St Nunn, or St Nonna, after whom the village is named, was the mother of St David, patron saint of Wales. It is supposed that her altar is preserved somewhere in the village. The Holy well also bears her name and like the one at St Cleer is thought to cure insanity.

The church is known as "The Cathedral of the Moor" and features a Norman font and a wonderful collection of carved pew ends dating back to the 16th century.

Trewint:

This little village was for many years cut in two by the busy A30. Now by-passed, it is a quiet place visited only by those making a pilgrimage to the little cottage down Duck Street. It was here in the mid 1700s that a local man, Digory Isbell, built an extension on to his home, so that John Wesley, the Methodist preacher, could have somewhere to stay whilst on his travels into deepest Cornwall. The cottage is now open to the public and contains fascinating displays on all things "methodical".

A Long Way from Home:

Sea shells on Bodmin Moor? At first I thought my eyes were deceiving me, but no, as I crossed a field I saw what appeared to be sand and sea shells on the closely cropped grass. Was this the result of a tremendous storm that had thrown debris this far inland, or perhaps a waterspout which had sucked sand up into

the sky and deposited it here, high on the moor? No, the reason was somewhat more prosaic: the farmer had recently spread his fields with sea sand to improve the ground, just as lime is often used elsewhere in the country – a practice which goes back centuries and is still carried out to this day.

right, to a gate into the next small field. Pass a ruined barn on your left before climbing steps in the bank into another large field, where you should head diagonally to your right to where the back of a lorry is being used as a makeshift barn. Go over the stile to the right of the "barn" and then follow the hedgerow on the left. The path swaps to the other side of the hedge through a gateway on the left as it proceeds through four fields, eventually crossing the last one to the road where you turn left. You have reached **Trewint**.

Leave Trewint by heading left down the old A30 towards Five Lanes. For those wishing to visit **Altarnun**, a footpath goes off on the left shortly after some cottages are passed. This follows the edge of fields before emerging onto the Altarnun road by way of some fine metal gates.

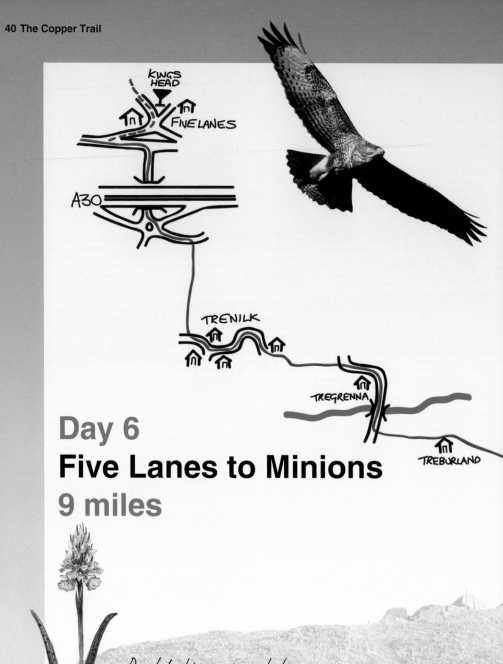

KINGS HEAD

FIVE LANES

A30

TRENILK

TREGRENNA

TREBURLAND

Day 6
Five Lanes to Minions
9 miles

Dactylorhiza maculata
HEATH SPOTTED - ORCHID
MOORLAND SPOTTED - ORCHID

The Kings Head at Five Lanes can be visited for refreshments, but otherwise follow the road signs for Bodmin taking you under the modern A30 to a roundabout. From here take the turning to Trevague (2nd left) and after a short distance go over a stile on the right. Now three fields have to be crossed. It is easy to spot the stiles, and soon you will reach the small hamlet of Trenilk. Turn left here and wind your way through the houses keeping an eye out for the old butter store on the left (it

looks a bit like a bus shelter!). The lane eventually ends at a private house, the footpath continuing between the buildings before turning right to a stile on the left. Stay close to the left hand hedge as you go through the next three fields with views over the Lynher Valley towards Fox Tor on the right. After the third field, the path goes over another stile and you will find the hedge on your right. Follow this until you reach a road.

The former Domesday manor of Tregrenna appears in front of you. Walk along the road past it and then follow it downhill to cross the infant **River Lynher**. Carry on up the lane a short distance until you reach a

NEWTON

TOLCARNE

STONAFORD

TREBARTHA

TO NORTH HILL

RIVER LYNHER

WITHEYBROOK

set of steps on the left which you climb into a field. Once in the field cross towards the telegraph pole and the green corrugated barn. Behind and to the left of the barn, the path exits onto the road. Turn left passing Treburland Farmhouse and then go over two stiles to the left of an old oak tree. The path now descends to the left of a hedge and

the remains of some buildings that were part of the **Treburland mining** operations which were active here up until World War II. Beyond the buildings, stepping stones cross a stream to a stile. Once over this, the path goes slightly left towards another oak tree and another stile.

The landscape now changes as the path enters a coniferous plantation, roughly following the power lines and weaving in between the trees before reaching another lane. Turn right here (don't take stile opposite) and after passing Heronford you will

find some steps on the left. Take care descending these as the gaps between steps are large. After crossing a small meadow more fir trees line the route but once through these you will find yourself back on the moor. A stile and steps are descended beside another grand oak. Turn left along the track/stream and ignore the arrow pointing left over the fence a few yards further on. Follow the footpath as it climbs slightly uphill and soon, where the path divides, fork right and follow the arrows.

Views of Dartmoor and the tree topped Tolcarne Tor can be seen to the left. Closer, in the woods across the valley, the ruins of Upton Castle dating from the 11th/12th

century can be found. Reaching a wall on your left, follow it above the fields to a gate. To the left of the gate is a boundary stone with the letter A carved into it. These stones stretch away up the hill to the west and out over the open moor. They mark part of the boundary between Altarnun

Trough or Apple Crusher?

and North Hill parish.

Go through the gate (not easy to open) and follow the track towards Clitters. Although the house is no longer lived in, it is obviously looked after and used at times. See if you can spot the serpents looking out of the wood.

The track continues past the house, winding around the edge of the fields and then climbs to the edge of the wood where you go through a gate. From here follow the wall as it descends under low trees to a gateway. Here the path turns into a sunken lane between high rocky banks dropping down to Tolcarne Farm, mentioned in the Domesday Book as Talgar.

At Tolcarne look out for the nice stone trough beside the path before heading off down the road ahead towards Stonaford, which is not much more than a few houses and a timber yard. Turn left here and follow the road as it gently descends into the valley. After once again crossing the River Lynher, the road climbs up to woodland where a footpath goes off to the right through the woods. This area is all part of the **Trebartha** estate and

River Lynher and the Withybrook:

If the Camel is the guardian of the western moor then the Lynher is the guardian of the east side. Forming on the high ground to the west of Trewint, it flows through East Cornwall joining the Tamar just below Saltash. The name is said to derive from "long lake" or "lake like" depending on which book you read.

The Withybrook is the main tributary of the Lynher and starts its life as the Withybrook Marsh, a no-go area to the west of Stowe's Hill. From there it flows northwards along the edge of Twelve Men's Moor before suddenly turning right below Trewortha Tor and tumbling down off the granite moorland through thick forestry to join the Lynher at Trewartha.

Treburland Mines:

All around the edge of Bodmin Moor little clusters of mines developed in the 1800's. Here at Treburland, as well as tin and copper, manganese and wolfram were mined. Wheal Annie is still marked on OS maps. Its sister mine, the amusingly named Wheal Flop, is not. By the 20th century the mines had amalgamated under the title Treburland Mine and worked up until the Second World War when 2,000 tons of tin and wolfram were brought to surface.

The celebrated British mineral collector Sir Arthur Russell made many visits to Treburland in the early 20th century. He identified over 30 different types of minerals in the area, many of which formed part of his collection of over 14,000 specimens, now part of the Natural History Museum in London.

Trebartha:

Though still a big estate, the glory days have long gone. It was acquired by a Norman knight shortly after the conquest and had passed by marriage or will down to the Rodd family who finally sold the estate in 1940. It was the Rodds that rebuilt Trebartha Hall and Squire Rodd was almost certainly the inspiration for Squire Bassett in du Maurier's "Jamaica Inn".

The hall no longer stands; it was demolished after WWII. It had been used as a Royal Army Medical Corps hospital but when they left, it was supposedly in such a state that it was easier to pull down than to repair.

Since 1940 when the Latham family bought the estate, it has been primarily run as a forestry based concern, hence all the fir plantations on this side of the moor. The grandeur of the original hall can only be guessed at, but if it is anything like the buildings that flank the road through the hamlet it must have been a fine house.

Twelve Men's Moor:

This unusual name dates back to the 13th century when the priory at Launceston made an agreement with the twelve tenants who farmed the area between the Withybrook and the Lynher. It includes the windswept tors of Kilmar, Hawk's, Trewortha, Bearah and Sharptor, some of the most rugged and beautiful scenery on the moor.

Henwood:

It is easy to forget as you stand here in the peace and quiet of the Cornish countryside that 150 years ago this village was at the centre of the industrial revolution. Up to 12 engine houses belched smoke from the hillside opposite, machinery toiled all

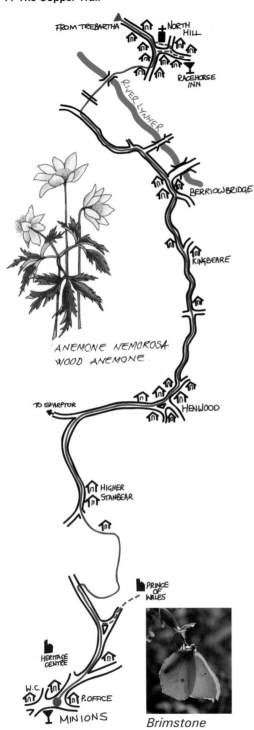

ANEMONE NEMOROSA
WOOD ANEMONE

although the main house no longer exists, there are still many fine buildings to be seen.

The short footpath cuts off a corner and when the road is rejoined, turn right and follow it past the hamlet of Trebartha. A sharp left hand bend leads to a long straight section of road into North Hill. Below you to the right, the River Lynher has suddenly become a proper river, joined, below Trebartha, by the waters of the **Withybrook**.

The quiet village of North Hill is reached where a diversion must be made if you are in need of refreshments. Go through the churchyard and down some old steps. Turn right, then left, and walk down the road past some interesting buildings to the Racehorse Inn.

On leaving the Inn, turn left back up the road and follow it to the junction with the road from Trebartha. Turn left again and go down the road

Brimstone

past the old Methodist chapel. Just below the chapel a footpath leaves the road on the right hand side. It winds between two houses before reaching a field where it descends to a stile into the woods, just left of the tall trees. You will soon hear the sound of the river as you cross a track and head for a bridge. There are in fact two bridges here; the first crosses a millstream whilst the second crosses the main river.

Leaving the river, the path climbs through the wood before some steps lead you into a field. Keep to your right as you climb up to a stile then

Sharp Tor

cross a farm track that leads to East Castick. Over another stile carry on upwards and you will eventually, after a long climb, emerge onto the road that leads up to **Twelve Men's Moor**. With rights of way few and far between on the high moor and despite many areas being described as "**Common Land**" the route must now follow the road by turning left and descending to Berriowbridge.

Here you meet the main Liskeard to Launceston road and great care must be taken. Do not turn left and go over the 17th century bridge

day, clanking and banging, and disease was rife in what would have been little more than a shanty town. To get an idea of what life was like up here, read the novel "Catch the Wind" by E.V. Thompson. It tells of the trials and tribulations of a miner's life here in the valley in the mid 1800s.

Common Land:

The term "common land" is often misunderstood. In the context of Bodmin Moor the term refers to the right of certain farmers and landowners to graze their animals on these common areas. Most of Bodmin Moor is in private ownership, even those areas known as common land, and it is interesting that the owner of the common land, known as The Lord of The Manor is (as far as I am aware), not usually allowed to graze his own animals upon it.

The "commoners" are farmers, with land usually adjacent to the common land, whose "Rights of Common" are determined by the area of land within their own farm, known as "inby" (pronounced "in-buy"), land. The amount of inby land determines the number of grazing units that the commoner is entitled to put out on the common. One grazing unit might, for instance, be one cow, which is equivalent perhaps, to one pony or four sheep or so many chickens or geese etc.

Recently an element of commerce has entered the system (people will always buy and sell anything won't they?). The commons rights were once inextricably tied to the particular farm (and the inby land) that they were historically attached to. But a recent court judgement has decreed that the rights themselves can be sold as a commodity which has meant that farmers who no longer use their Common Rights are able to sell them on to whosoever they wish. It is fair to say that modern attempts to legislate a system of land management which originated in medieval times has been less than satisfactory and the 1965 Commons Registration Act in particular, and its procedure for registration left a lot to be desired. It is likely that there will be many more court cases before the wider issues of management and access to the commons are resolved.

Commoner's rights can also include the right of "Turbery" – the right to cut peat for fuel, "Pannage" – the right to turn pigs out into a wood to eat the acorns and beechmast, "Piscary" – the right to take fish from lakes or rivers and "Estovers" – the right to take bracken, furze and I think, fallen branches etc.

Phoenix United and the Prince of Wales Mine:

Little remains to the untrained eye of what was the largest mine in the area, except for the odd pile of masonry covered in cotoneaster. The lower part, rich in heathers, gorse and rhododendron bushes, contrasts heavily with the barren wasteland you reach at the top. Here nothing grows on the mineral rich waste tips where amateur geologists can sometimes be seen hunting for treasures. The area is now a Site of Special Scientific Interest (SSSI) and is home to mosses that grow no-where else in the world, as well as colonies of bats that roost in the adits draining the abandoned mines.

The Prince of Wales Mine was built in 1907 to tap into the by then closed down Phoenix mines. Although much money was spent on building the mine, no ore of any value was brought out and by 1914 it had closed, never to reopen. Over the last 10 years or so the buildings have been tidied up and made safe.

but follow the road between the houses to the next turning on the right. Take this and climb steeply upwards, the sunken lane cutting out sunlight in all but a few places. Several minor tracks branch off at intervals but keep on the road until the T-junction is reached at Kingbeare. Here you get a great view of Sharp Tor towering above you, belying its quite lowly height of 378 meters (1209 ft). Turn right and continue along the road passing an abandoned quarry to the crossroads at Blackcoombe Farm. The track on the right would lead you up to Bearah Tor and its quarry, where stone is still worked by the Piper family.

Your route continues along the road, passing a riding centre before dropping down into the village of **Henwood**. Here a bench on the "green" makes a fine resting point with views to the south. Leave the village heading in a westerly direction, uphill towards Minions. Passing the turning to Sharptor, the road dips before climbing again

between the trees. Halfway up stop, and turn round: Sharp Tor once again towers over the surrounding countryside.

Continue uphill to the cottages at Stanbear where a bridleway drops off on the left. Follow this down to a footbridge beside a large wall. The wall once held back water used to power the various mining concerns in the valley below you, the main one being the Darley Slime Works. This was where the waste from the mines was sorted through to extract every last scrap of tin or copper. Follow the wall around to the right to where the path climbs up onto the former **Phoenix United Mine** site. Little remains to be seen by the untrained eye but this area was a hive of activity in the 1800s. The path weaves its way between gorse and cotoneaster until it reaches a barren area where waste from the mining operations holds back growth. You should be able to see the famous **Cheesewring** rock formation perched on the side of the hill high above you to the right. At

The Prince of Wales Mine

the top of the barren area the path divides in front of a fenced off shaft. Turn right and follow the signposts down into the valley. The path soon climbs again, curving round between more shafts to reach the road beside the remains of an engine house. Turn left here and follow the road to Minions.

Over to your left you can see the remains of the **Prince of Wales mine** with the patchworked farm lands of East Cornwall beyond it. On a clear day the tors of Dartmoor should be visible on the eastern horizon. The road soon reaches the outskirts of **Minions** and passes a large car park on the right. Beyond the car park the engine house that can be seen is now a heritage centre for the area. It is not staffed, but features plenty of interesting information on what can be seen and done within a short walk from the village.

Take care as you follow the road into the centre of the village where the post office/shop/tea rooms can be found alongside the Cheesewring Hotel and the Hurlers Halt teashop.

For those of you who started the walk in Minions, well done! I hope you have enjoyed it and will go on to explore the rest of the moor.

The Cheesewring and Stowe's Hill:

Alongside Jamaica Inn and Dozmary Pool most visitors to Bodmin Moor head for the Cheesewring. This tower of naturally balanced stones has drawn people to the southern edge of the moor since time immemorial. Although it is one particular tower that gets all the publicity, there are several other 'cheesewrings' atop Stowe's Hill that are worth viewing. Their origins can be traced back 280 million years to when the molten granite rock that now forms the backbone of Cornwall and Devon, solidified. Later, when the Ice Ages ended, the solid rocks found themselves standing tall while all the loose rocks got carried downhill with the melting soil. Over the many years since, the wind and rain have eaten into the fault lines in the rock to produce these strange forms.

The name 'Cheesewring' comes from the fact that these rocks

resemble the bags of apple pulp used for making cider. These are known locally as cheeses and when piled on top of each other in a press, form a similar shape.

The other feature that makes Stowe's Hill a fascinating place to visit is the Neolithic hillfort that surrounds the summit. It is in two parts, with the higher, smaller enclosure circling the top of the hill and taking in many of the cheesewring formations. To the north of this lies the larger enclosure on slightly lower ground. Whereas the higher enclosure has no sign of habitation, this lower area is covered in circles of stone that may have been sites for huts or just clearings for tents. There are also burial sites and a sunken entranceway to be explored here, that could date back over 6000 years.

Moor Walks

You may or may not be aware that The Best of Bodmin Moor have already published three booklets of short circular walks, on and around Bodmin Moor.

Between them these three publications provide you with a walk in each of the eighteen parishes which make up Bodmin Moor. The walks are distributed in each booklet in such a way, that wherever you are in the area, you will not be far away from the start of a walk.

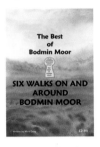 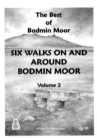 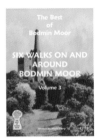

with walks in:	with walks in:	with walks in:
St Breward	Warleggan	St Tudy
St Clether	Lewannick	Altarnun
St Neot	Michaelstow	Cardinham
Blisland	St Ive	Linkinhorne
St Cleer	Helland	Camelford
North Hill	Advent	Davidstow

Please help **us** to help **you**....

We would be very grateful for **any** feedback about your experiences on The Copper Trail. Please email **feedback@coppertrail.co.uk** with your anecdotes, gripes (hopefully, not too many), or comments. We also have an on-line questionnaire available via **www.bobm.info.** Your response will be kept in the strictest confidence and will help us to maintain and improve the route and the nearby services in the future.

And Finally.......................

If you are visiting Bodmin Moor from out of the area (and indeed if you are intending to walk the Copper Trail in one go), then you may need some accommodation. Please visit **www.bobm.info** and follow the links to find high quality, independently inspected, bed & breakfast, self catering or campsite accommodation in our area.

Paul Glendell, © The Countryside Agency